END
of the
WORLD

END
of the
WORLD

Great Hope!

A seer

Library of Congress Control Number: 2023921523
ISBN: Hardcover   978-1-6698-8813-0
               Softcover   978-1-6698-8812-3
               eBook   978-1-6698-8811-6

Print information available on the last page.

Rev. date: 09/28/2023

To order additional copies of this book, contact:
Xlibris
AU TFN: 1 800 844 927 (Toll Free inside Australia)
AU Local: (02) 8310 8187 (+61 2 8310 8187 from outside Australia)
www.Xlibris.com.au
Orders@Xlibris.com.au
837998

CONTENTS

PREFACE

Behold, he cometh with clouds; and every eye shall see him, and they also which pierced him: and all kindreds of the earth shall wail because of him. Even so, Amen. (Revelation 1:7 KJV)

Yet all Jesus asks is that we humble ourselves, repent of evil and arrogancy and follow and obey him.

Interlude

There are terrible and great things taking place in the world since I started writing this book. More recently there are more earthquakes of far greater magnitude. You do not know when your time to die is coming. So be ready to meet your maker. His name is Jesus Christ. He died for you on that cross. All you must do is accept his sacrifice for you when he died on the cross. Believe he was raised from the dead and start to live a new life of righteousness. What is righteousness? It is a life of living not in the ways of the world in general but of a clear conscience of ones thoughts and actions and most importantly God' spirit leading all this.

If you will get yourself a simple Christian Bible and ask God to guide you, you will find the answers to all your questions on what to do next. Here is the next most important thing you must do, and that is to ask God to forgive your wrongdoing, be baptised and then receive the Holy Spirit. These are things generally done in a Church, so that will be your next mission, to find a Christian Church that follows the truth and let them lead you in your new journey. In the mean time there is a lot to know however so if you seek God with all your heart mind and soul you will find all the answers you are looking for. Simply get down on your knees and pray and ask God for forgiveness and the way forward every day.

Jesus saith unto him, I am the way, the truth, and the life: no man cometh unto the Father, but by me. (John 14:6)

Seek ye the Lord, all ye meek of the earth, which have wrought his judgment; seek righteousness, seek meekness: it may be ye shall be hid in the day of the Lord's anger. (Zephaniah 2:3)

You must remember however to seek God every day yourself as times are going to get tough as you have no doubt noticed. In Luke 18:1 it states:

'1 And he spake a parable unto them to this end, that men ought always to pray, and not to faint;'

That is, not to give up.

These things I have spoken unto you, that in me ye might have peace. In the world ye shall have tribulation: but be of good cheer; I have overcome the world. (John 16:33 KJV)

Peace I leave with you, my peace I give unto you: not as the world giveth, give I unto you. Let not your heart be troubled, neither let it be afraid. (John 14:2 7KJV)

Teaching them to observe all things whatsoever I have commanded you: and, lo, I am with you alway, even unto the end of the world. Amen. (Matthew 28:20 KJV)

Do not lose sight of the promise of God in that he has said "I will never leave you nor forsake you." (Hebrews 13:5 KJV)

'The time period most of this book covers is from Jan 2019 through end of 2030.

Due to delays on my part the book has come out late but I want to warn the world none the less.

I stated that I did not wish to discuss the book until 2030. That is still the case'.

INTRODUCTION

Dear Reader,

I write today with great hope and bright expectations of the future: there is in me, as with multitudes, that hope of restoration for the now here on earth and the hereafter by way of God's glory and grace.

I have a great challenge of choice for you. As you read this collection of documentaries, I hope you will find in them the weight of evidence to allow yourself to follow the Lord Jesus Christ. As it is reported of him saying,

'Enter ye in at the strait gate: for wide is the gate, for broad is the way, that leadeth to destruction, and many there be which go in thereat. Because strait is the gate, and narrow is the way, which leadeth unto life, and few there be that find it' (Matthew 7:13–14, KJV).

THE FAITHFUL

The way of the Lord is most often simple and non-glamorous from the outside looking in, even to the point where people choose loss and suffering and even death over freedom that compromises their chosen faith walk. As we have seen over the last twenty years, the acceptance of a change of religion or politics would mean a crude form of habeas corpus and a chance at freedom – or possibly a grant of passage to a safe haven or being spared from a brutal and cruel death.

Those I am speaking of, however, choose rather to hold to their convictions and have paid by limb and even life. Why would they? The world has become extremely wicked. Masses starve and some go naked and homeless. Many are subject to war and terror, yet ultra-wealthy persons continue the machinery and industry that supply conflict and death. So their money and power will not save them in the end.

There are those among us who live their lives with little complaint and never ask for more than that which is sufficient for their daily needs. They live within their means and where they can give to others and to causes that are worthwhile to them. They follow the words of advice from other simple and good people and would not take a shoelace in payment. They hope for an eternal reward to simply be accepted in God's family both in the now and the next – to be with God in his paradise and forever with him, often a seeming faraway promise. Without them, the world would not run as there are minions of them who volunteer, never requiring reward but seeing it as their duty to give back to the world. Not only in Christianity, people of great kindness all over the world do all they can to ameliorate what greed and lust has yielded us. Their reward will be to sit with Jesus and have all their tears wiped away.

THE WICKED

There will be great revealing of corporate criminals in the midst. They will be shockingly revealed to most seeing many of them the world esteems highly. Evidence will be delivered to honest and deserving officers so clearly that only the most foolish and manipulated media outlets will continue to hide the corruption. Many career journalists and broadcasters will run for cover when they are faced with answering the embarrassing truth that they lied to all of us. Giants will fall. Both the doers of wrong and the concealers of wrong.

TO BEGIN

Now I will share with you messages and accounts of dreams and visions which will not only add to the mystery of such faith but also, I hope, give weight to your deciding in favour of this faith. Though possibly through suffering, you may see the joy that is set before you, both for now and the life hereafter – for 'the Joy of the Lord is our strength'. Nehemiah 8:10

The debate and discourse that likely will follow have thought long and hard about. Here in these pages is what I must publish as time is short. I have weighed and considered each topic through joy and duress, ecstasy and sorrow. Of late, people of all walks of life feel that they must be answerable to every facet of media and enquiry. People such as myself choose not to. Only years ago, people would be in touch by letters, telegrams, and phone calls. One had time to consider their position before making a statement or making a decision, great or small. The newspapers and magazines were the only form of exposure, mostly for people of notoriety. Today our politicians and leaders spend a great deal of their time facing the media barrage. Interviewers are often disrespectful and have no real understanding of the questions they are asking. Sessions in front of the camera, live or recorded, are often scathing and demeaning for anyone in authority.

Every person carrying responsibility in all facets of life and office should take time in preparing their statements wisely so as to avoid being branded as something other than they intended or provoked to state something they will later regret. We all would do well to do likewise. Please understand that I have not changed the text of any of the messages from the time of writing, so the wording may appear out of context with the present time. I commend your conscience to God.

Note: These messages were written a while ago, and I am doing my best to relay the importance of each of the messages, which were all new to me at the time of writing. The most crucial component of this book is to believe the Gospel and believe in Jesus and that you must repent of your sins and seek knowledge directly from God and ask for direction daily, hourly, and sometimes even moment by moment to navigate what is to come. So pray, very simply and to that point. Like the disciple Peter when going down into the depths cried "Lord, save me!" Matthew 14:30. Never doubt that Jesus Christ is able to see you and a way for you and your family. Put your total trust in him and don't be afraid; don't get angry. Both of those emotions will stilt your better judgement. Your mind needs to remain clear and calm. You can know peace even as the world around you crumbles.

This, I assure you as so many have walked through terrible troubles and conflict yet known that God is walking with them. If you are blessed to have an old Christian you can talk to, they can shed light on the many ways they found comfort and help through war and trial simply by praying and asking help from God and their faith and trust in Jesus Christ. The other great signpost of our time is that 'COVID is at an end!' Don't be dragged away from this truth; God will protect you and heal you if you will put your total trust in him.

THE AUTHOR

Warning to the Ultra Wealthy

There is an opportunity for those the very wealthy to help in what seems to be a hopeless plight. There are a multitude of organisations for any of us to support. Here is a basic list:

Medicines Sans Frontiers	St Vincint de Paul	Destiny Rescue
Rescue.org	UNICEF	Anti Slavery International
Red Cross	World Vision	Stop the Traffik
Red Crescent	Walk Free	Human Trafficking Foundation
Compassion	The Freedom Fund	Hope for Justice
Salvation Army	International Labour Organisation	

There are many other worthy organisations in the world today and they are easy to find. Even in your neighbourhood or people you already know. You will find plenty of them so take your pick only do it quick. There will be a reckoning of those with much who do not help to alleviate the suffering and affliction of others nearby. Perhaps you are reading this and laughing as you are profiting from slavery, trafficking or exploitation. I strongly urge you to amend your ways as you will shortly feel the sting of an angry God. The time has come.

To those who profit from industries such as weapons, illegal weapons, drugs money laundering, human trafficking, illegal drugs and generally any questionable activity I give you this opportunity to repent and change the course of your life: Follow Jesus, ask for forgiveness, give forgiveness, cry out to God for help.

For those of you who know of such things be honest, vigilant and truthful. God is sending a special task force to earth to deal with corruption. The technology is way beyond anything on earth. The intelligence officers have the ability to walk through walls and thick concrete bunkers and vaults. They can even see straight into your hard drive. The consequences of wicked works is coming fast. For those mega wealthy persons who operate legally consider upping your giving willingly and joyfully to these or any worthy organisations. Otherwise it may not go so well for you. For those receiving and distributing that which others have given likewise conduct your affairs as though the angels are looking over your shoulder. (They are there to help.)

And he shall judge among many people, and rebuke strong nations afar off; and they shall beat their swords into plowshares, and their spears into pruninghooks: nation shall not lift up a sword against nation, neither shall they learn war any more. Micah 4:3 KJV

For unto whomsoever much is given, of him shall be much required: and to whom men have committed much, of him they will ask the more. Luke 12:48 (b) KJV

FIERCE WRATH

This is one of the most recent messages I have received. It is one that I hope Australia and the world will take notice of.

A Prophecy (28/8/21)

To all who hope in the redemption of Jesus Christ and those who don't, there will be much trouble if the governments of this world do not heed the warnings of the Almighty God. In times past, when God told any people or nation to repent, if they did not, these consequences were brought upon them, some or all:

- Drought
- Famine
- Floods
- Fires
- Earthquakes
- Enemy invasion

This is the word I have heard from the Almighty Spirit of Jesus Christ:

Prepare for the fierce wrath of the Lord Almighty!

18 And there were voices and thunders and [lightning]; and there was a great earthquake such as was not since men were upon the earth, so mighty an earthquake and so great.

19 And the great city was divided into three parts, and
the cities of the nations fell: and great Babylon came
in remembrance before God, to give unto her the cup
of the wine of the fierceness of his wrath.

(Revelation 16:18–20)

Leaders of both private organisations and the government
must hear and yield to the reasonable request of the Lord God
Almighty and do those things which preserve the life and freedom
of all people. You must shut down all abortion clinics and quash all
paedophile networks and sex-trafficking operations, including child
pornography, as an imperative action. There is much corruption and
collaboration of these wicked operations with various aspects of the
supposed respectable government and public organisations. Time
has run out, and all will see the beginning of what will be a severe
and total judgement of all who disobey the gospel of our Lord Jesus
Christ. I need only mention every other crime, wrongdoing, and
injustice that we are all aware of. Those crimes mentioned at the
top of this paragraph are well in the power of governments and their
people to effect necessary change and are among the worst. God is
watching, and you will be spared or chastised accordingly as you
act. Take heed. In line with this will be the mother of all storms
in many cities not limited to but including our own Sydney, NSW.
Evacuation will be necessary but not in the first instance. If these
mandates are not followed, more severe storms will come.

CONVERGENCE

I would have placed all the messages in order with this one last. The reason I have placed it early in the manuscript is that there has been a recent earthquake near Melbourne, Australia. In the narrative of the Book of Revelation, there is mention of those who will be given the power to shut up heaven so that 'there be no rain'. Along with this, they will 'call down fire from above, and no man will be able to harm them'. We who believe, though riddled with faults, hold to all these writings and can see the end now looming. It is with joy and trepidation that we consider the laws and motions that governments and world governments are making. We can see the time of judgement looming, as Jesus told us:

> [28] Now learn a parable of the fig tree; when her branch is yet tender and putteth forth leaves, ye know that summer is near. [29] So ye in like manner, when ye shall see these things come to pass, know that it is nigh, even at the doors. (Mark 13:28–29, KJV)

For as long as I have believed in Jesus, I have been on a journey of how to show the love of God to those around us. So guided by God, I began praying for rain as I believe God had asked me to. Recently, we have been abundantly blessed as truly, we all see the Murray–Darling basin filling up! It is cause to rejoice and give God our thanks. There was much prayer and intercession for this. In the same way the rains have come, God wishes his people to ask for the rain of revival upon our lands and nation. Now we see too much rain that harvesting is difficult and crops could be lost, but any farmer can go out to their fields and ask for the sunshine they need with a humble heart, and it will be granted. Try it quietly on your own. You will be pleasantly surprised. First Nation people and farmers of all nations understand the importance of our relationship with the earth. People of great power who only work the land from afar make decisions that are good for their wealth and control, not for the equity and longevity of the earth and people.

This work of prayer is ongoing, and the revival is almost here. I asked whether I should call for earthquakes, as it states in many books of the Bible. The answer came back very clearly as a no, for while this period of his grace extends, his desire is to show all people his love by giving the rain and the fruits of the field for all. I do reinforce that if people do not repent, earthquakes and worse events will occur within these next eight years. By mid-2028, tremors will begin and increase with frequency and intensity. The wickedness of some has meant drought and all the associated sorrows of famine and fire. There has been a great intervention of rain for Australia all because of the great prayers of many, all desiring healing and revival in our land and in the world at large. As we all have seen, the drought has broken as multitudes have not relented in asking for God's kindness and healing for our land, and so many farmers have been saved in more ways than merely a return to agriculture. His love is in this world everywhere, and there is so much more that he will do if only mankind will return to him in repentance and humility. It remains to be seen if the major powers of the world and the United Nations will acknowledge the true and living God. However, here is the mandate: as we have cried out our prayers to God for rain and for our nation to repent, we continually remind ourselves of this ancient promise found in the Bible.

[13] If I shut up heaven that there be no rain, or if I command the locusts to devour the land, or if I send pestilence among my people; [14] if my people who are called by my name shall humble themselves and pray and seek my face and turn from their wicked ways; then I will hear from heaven and will forgive their sin and will heal their land. (2 Chronicles 7:13–14)

A SIMPLE COVENANT

Even if you have not received much rain until now, do go out into your paddocks or holdings and lift your hands to God. Conversely, if you have had too much rain, ask for forgiveness for whatever you may have done wrong and set yourself right with God. Receive Jesus into your heart; take your family and do it together. Then ask for rain (or dry), and it will surely come. Your joy will also begin. You can work with your neighbours as well. God wishes to bless you. If no one else will believe, they will certainly acknowledge the flourishing farm that yours will become, and as we all know, time and seasons come around again. They will be more considerate of your message the next year!

A dispensation of grace and forgiveness is on Australia for a period of ten years in total. Two seasons have passed since the drought broke. There will be eight more years of good seasons; however, in that time, if our nation does not yield to God, the earthquakes will start. There will be tremors of increasing magnitude and frequency. It will be better to move away from the major cities, such as Sydney and especially Melbourne and Canberra. (It is interesting to note that the ABC radio frequency for Canberra is 666.) If the Government of Australia and these states do not turn away from the many evils that have been adopted as normality, it is likely that these three cities will be no more. At that time, Australia will become extremely vulnerable and most likely will be occupied under another nation's directives – effectively invaded. They will have no problem letting you suffer with the unimaginable (unimaginable especially in this country) famine and hunger and massive housing shortages, to say the least. Do pause to consider all this.

You can make your own covenant with God, and there are many testimonies to be found online of farmers who have spoken that above scripture or many of the other promises that God made to the ancient nation of Israel when they were also departing from the ways of God, only if they would return to him. There is much to look forward to – if the nations and this nation repent of all their sins, not limited to but especially those in that message on the page preceding this one. God is looking for an effort on our behalf to show that we are sincere in our efforts to right the wrongs that are so obvious to most of us.

People of all walks of life will suddenly be forced to acknowledge that all the basics we have taken for granted will become scarce and the foremost priority even for those who now consider themselves well off. Just as the wealthy on the ship Titanic could find no leverage with their money at the point of sinking, so will it be when nature, by the hand of God's fury, takes away all food, shelter, and clothing; thus, everyone's needs are the same in such circumstances.

Atheist Scientist

There is a leading scientist/athiest, this is the message I have regarding him: his time is short, and so he will shortly meet his maker. Further, there will be a point at which he will dispute with someone of faith, as he has done in the past. However, this time, he will be unable to speak for thirty days. It will be a sign to him and all about him. There will be more yet to his story after this. We pray for his salvation.

Famous Naturalist

The same situation as above however he is nearer to his end. We hope he reconsiders the faith he knows so well.

Mother of All Storms

Sydney, Australia, will receive the greatest of all storms in its known history. This will be a clear and utter destructive wave throughout all the major suburbs of the city, and unless many repent of their major sins, it will take a long time recovering. So close down all the abortion clinics and other places of vice to allay the judgement of the Almighty God. Other cities of the world face similar consequences, yet if they will repent and return to the loving arms of the Saviour, these disasters will not be sent. An early warning of the storm will be evident. As he has said; 'He makes a way where there is no way. He frustrates the tokens of the liars. He sets the solitary in families'. Pray with all your heart to know what to do and where to go or stay. If you serch for stories of people who sought God in terrible crisis you will see how they were spared the terrible consequences that might possibly have been.

CORONAVIRUS IS AT AN END! PART I (14/4/2020)

I wish to convey the message I received prior to this date, approximately 8 March 2020, some five weeks ago. It is in regard to the current disease crisis, as stated above.

Over my lifetime, when I feel that God is giving me a message, it is a profound dream or simply a strong sense that I should speak to someone or a Bible verse for me or others. I rarely ask God about the future; anytime people or news reports predict doom and gloom, I simply refer to all that Jesus himself stated on the future and how we should deal with it. Otherwise, it can grieve me so terribly that I become as some of the prophets who were beside themselves and could only languish in thought and were not able to do any other useful thing! These are and were the messages of the ancient prophets dealing with matters of life and death.

Five major consequences are listed upon a nation that forgets God or rebels against his laws:

- Famine, resulting from drought. He will withhold the rain, and this is always accompanied by higher-than-normal temperatures.
- Fire, also resulting from the lack of rain and combined with high temperatures, as we know so well in Australia.

- Flood, the natural turnaround from drought. The water runs off the dry land until the earth can absorb the moisture. The storms are also a reminder that the earth is in God's control.
- Earthquakes, from tremors through to devastating quakes that will flatten most manmade structures.
- Enemy invasion, the final step when there is absolutely no other measure left as all possible remedies are exhausted.

At the end of the world, we are told, 'The wicked shall be turned into hell and all the nations that forget God' (Psalms 9:17), and as we know so well, 'it is appointed unto men once to die but after this the judgment' (Hebrews 9:27). Those who understand all this, take heed of the message to fear and tremble before God.

My flesh trembleth for fear of thee; and I am afraid of thy judgments. Psalms 119:120

Most days, I am content to deal with daily affairs and leave the rest up to the Almighty God. However, images and messages have often been indelibly printed on my mind. I have been sought out to be shown things, and I must share them with as many people as possible. I have had momentary interventions whereby my train of thought has been less than godly and interrupted by a bump on the head, some other jolt or physical event, a near miss while driving in traffic, or some other thing which highlights the moment and causes me to examine my thoughts more wisely though momentarily. God wants to get my attention as such moments are serious and action is needed. God gently reminds me to get away from perilous thoughts (in my more stubborn times). I know God has used such a simple method of reproof to get my attention if I am going astray in my mind and then usually reminds me of all the blessings in my life and to be thankful, but this message I'm about to share was simply 'there'.

I cannot say anything major like a dream came with it, simply that it was there.

About five weeks ago, there was this in my mind, not foremost nor way back but simply a bright thought: 'This disease is manmade. Therefore, it will not last long, only two days.' I was not sure of what 'two days' meant; however, it had something to do with the time frame, though short, of how long COVID-19 would be among us. There have been approximately two months of the worst of the coronavirus, and that includes the present. Looking at the news, it appears to me that Australia is very close to having the disease under control, with reports of zero new infections yesterday in all states, excluding NSW. The 'two' may be two months. A Bible verse also came to me as plainly as the message itself, and it is the one from the book of John, Chapter 3, verses 14 and 15: 'And as Moses lifted up the serpent in the wilderness, even so must the Son of man be lifted up: that whosoever believeth in him should not perish but have eternal life'.

Here, we have one of the most important messages from Jesus and a principle that stands throughout time in that all those who 'look up' will see their deliverance if they do so with a sincere motive and a humble heart and persistent prayer:

[2] Looking unto Jesus, the author and finisher of our faith; who, for the joy that was set before him, endured the cross, despising the shame, and is set down at the right hand of the throne of God. (Hebrews 12:2, KJV)

The 'serpent' that Jesus mentions is from the book of Numbers:

[9] And Moses made a serpent of brass and put it upon a pole, and it came to pass that if a serpent had bitten any man when he beheld the serpent of brass, he lived. (Numbers 21:9, KJV)

Like us, the people of Israel were dying as a result of their own actions in that they knew very well not to speak against God and his chosen leader, with these people having witnessed the greatest of miracles that any people had ever seen, authoritatively facilitated by Moses on God's behalf. We have been plagued by those meddling with things they don't understand, or if they do, they deliberately release it upon the public, also speaking by their actions against God and his prophets. Scientists and pharmaceutical corporations deliberately put themselves above God and disregard all pleas to cease and desist. Rather, they vigorously pursue inhumane and heinous experiments, though they have been asked to be respectful of human and animal life by many community groups.

Therefore, the message is for this purpose: God wants us to know that the coronavirus was not from him, but we can nonetheless look to him for our healing and deliverance, and in this case, we will be seeing multitudes of miraculous healings from this disease. As those bitten by 'fiery serpents' and who looked upon the bronze serpent were able to live, so also will all those who look to the crucified Saviour, who was lifted up on the cross, be saved from the consequences of their own sin and, especially at this time, be saved from the coronavirus.

There is nevertheless a part for us all to play. At the end of every plague in Egypt, Moses had to pray or cry out to God to make it stop. No one else among all the people of Israel, the Egyptians, or any other race had the courage or authority from God to do so. Jesus has been given all power from the Father:

[26] And he that overcometh and keepeth my works unto the end, to him will I give power over the nations. [27] And he shall rule

them with a rod of iron; as the vessels of a potter shall they be broken to shivers: even as I received of my Father. (Revelation 2:26–27)

[18] All power is given unto me in heaven and earth. [19] Go ye therefore and teach all nations, baptising them in the name of the Father and of the Son and of the Holy Ghost: [20] teaching them to observe all things whatsoever I have commanded you: and lo, I am with you always, even unto the end of the world. Amen. (Matthew 28:18–20)

We have just celebrated Easter, and the Jews have just celebrated Passover. The set time of remembrance is right about now, and I encourage you all to pray and fast and declare loudly the deliverance of our time – Jesus Christ, the risen saviour for all time – and now especially in this plague that has taken so many lives. We have also been called to be the heralds of this unction from the Almighty. Not many will want to declare this message, but those who do this witness will serve to give weight to what is happening on earth at this time and help many to enter the kingdom of God – more simply, know God as your friend and helper.

[1] The Lord is my light and my salvation; whom shall I fear? the Lord is the strength of my life; of whom shall I be afraid? Psalm 27:1 KJV

When Jesus ministered he was always inviting all people of all nations and walks of life to enter the Kingdom of God. When talking about sudden death as in the 18 people who died in Siloam he stated this:

Think ye that they were sinners above all men that dwelt in Jerusalem?

5 I tell you, Nay: but, except ye repent, ye shall all likewise perish.

Luke 13:4-5 KJV

Recent Earthquake in Turkey Syria

I know this next passage may garner shock and offence seeing what is taking place in Turkey and Syria. I had no idea such an earthquake would come other than obviously I have had forewarning in the general sense and for the whole world, please turn to Jesus Christ and pray. This book is not only about punishment but much more repentence to salvation and therefore forgiveness. Death may be iminent but God wants you to seek Him, have your sins forgiven and be taken to Heaven when you die. This story is for example only and to encourage leaders and nations to put their whole hearted trust in The God and Father of our Lord Jesus Christ and turn away from the terrible evils that have become infused in our world.

Pray simple prayers, as the man on the cross next to Jesus cross stated:

"Lord when you come into your Kingdom remember me" Then Jesus said "This day you will be with me in paradise."

Please repent and ask forgiveness from God, forgive your enemies or those who have hurt you. We will all die sooner or later, and when we do, we need to have forgiven all those around us so that God can forgive us.

Matthew 18:21-35

21 Then came Peter to him, and said, Lord, how oft shall my brother sin against me, and I forgive him? till seven times?

22 Jesus saith unto him, I say not unto thee, Until seven times: but, Until seventy times seven.

23 Therefore is the kingdom of heaven likened unto a certain king, which would take account of his servants.

24 And when he had begun to reckon, one was brought unto him, which owed him ten thousand talents.

25 But forasmuch as he had not to pay, his lord commanded him to be sold, and his wife, and children, and all that he had, and payment to be made.

26 The servant therefore fell down, and worshipped him, saying, Lord, have patience with me, and I will pay thee all.

27 Then the lord of that servant was moved with compassion, and loosed him, and forgave him the debt.

28 But the same servant went out, and found one of his fellowservants, which owed him an hundred pence: and he laid hands on him, and took him by the throat, saying, Pay me that thou owest.

29 And his fellowservant fell down at his feet, and besought him, saying, Have patience with me, and I will pay thee all.

30 And he would not: but went and cast him into prison, till he should pay the debt.

31 So when his fellowservants saw what was done, they were very sorry, and came and told unto their lord all that was done.

32 Then his lord, after that he had called him, said unto him, O thou wicked servant, I forgave thee all that debt, because thou desiredst me:

33 Shouldest not thou also have had compassion on thy fellowservant, even as I had pity on thee?

34 And his lord was wroth, and delivered him to the tormentors, till he should pay all that was due unto him.

Now I hope you will do me a favour and read the Second Book of Kings, Chapter 13, paying particular attention to verses 14 to 19. In here, the narrative is about the usual kings who went after all the things God forbade them to. There was this one king who arose amidst the malaise who actually wanted to do what was right before God: Joash. He tearfully sought out the prophet Elisha to know how to defeat one of their nation's enemies, and Elisha, though deathly sick, symbolically placed his hands on the king's hands while he fired an arrow out the window (15, 16, and 17). Elisha stated that this would be a sign of deliverance from the Syrians, who were greatly oppressing the Israelites at that time. The direction of the arrow was important, eastward toward the Syrian nation. Then it was time for Joash to agree and participate in a symbolic action and confirm that he would obey God's voice through Elisha and seal his acceptance by an action.

In verse 18, Elisha instructed Joash to take arrows and smite the ground with them, which he did but only three times. In verse 19, Elisha was furious as there was clearly a lack of purposeful determination in Joash; Elisha had prophetically opened the door of deliverance for Joash, yet he took only what many of us would consider a fair share. God and Elisha wanted him to take control and defeat the Syrians completely, but Joash was afraid of many things and didn't go as far as he should have. At the end of the chapter, Joash defeated them three times; however, later on, the Syrians bothered Israel many times.

We all have our part to play in a miracle, and how willingly we push is proportional to how great the result will be. Shout it out – 'Jesus Christ is risen! And COVID is at an end!'

CORONAVIRUS IS AT AN END!
PART II (31/7/21)

I must declare that which the Lord my God is strongly urging me to speak. I will give the first part of this message that I received back in 2020 just after Easter. This message I'm about to share was simply 'there'. I cannot say anything major like a dream came with it, simply that it was there.

About five weeks ago, there was this in my mind, not foremost nor way back but simply a bright thought: 'This disease is manmade. Therefore, it will not last long, only two days.' The coronavirus is nearing its end. This will occur late this year and be finalised by March 2022. I will declare the end of the coronavirus at that time to signify what God has said. God spoke to me, and I understand that at the end of two years, the coronavirus will have failed to accomplish the end for which it was created. This will also include the 'delta variant' that the creators had hoped will carry the devastation forth beyond imaginable control efforts by human health professionals and mercy workers.

The ideology of all who believe they can act as 'gods', deciding on who will die and who will live, has been deemed by the true and living God as exceeding their authority. They will be judged for this.

The method now being used to control the masses by fear will have no grounds after that point in time. It will be clung to by all the usual media and health representatives for as long as possible. If you want truth and freedom to remain in our nation, then set your mind on God so that his great and marvellous deeds, signs, and wonders will flow around our nation in these coming days as well as the general peace and prosperity we have known here in Australia for a long time. God has sent our nation abundant rain. Rejoice in all this and all the blessings of this great land and pray and seek God that we may love the Lord our God with all our hearts, minds, and souls and that we will truly love our neighbours as ourselves!

Reading Suggestions:

— Psalms 23
— The Lord's Prayer: Matthew 6:9, Luke 11:2

Grace be to all those who love our Lord Jesus Christ in sincerity. Amen. Ephesians 6:24.

GOVERNMENT MAKING LAWS OF WRONG (7/8/2021)

The Lord has heard and will judge you: Because you have not heard my word concerning the children, I will judge you and your companions. You will hear from me and know that it is I who have kindled a fire in your house and that your decrees written are not by me. Your decrees will burn to the ground even as you seek to strengthen them. The people of the land will rise up and throw you out of your place, and wherever you propose to place a foot to establish a sanctuary, there will be fire unless you repent, do not kill the babies or the young innocents, otherwise you will have chaos in place of government. You have two years to remedy the situation, or I will judge you, and even before I do, your decrees will burn to the ground. Listen to your conscience. If you sit quietly, you will hear my voice, pray to me in your boardrooms. Then I will guide you and peace, true peace will ensue. There is much good I wish to bestow upon you and the people of the World, but you must listen and obey me.

We are told in 1 Timothy 2:1–4 (KJV),

[1] I exhort therefore that, first of all, supplications, prayers, intercessions, and giving of thanks be made for all men; [2] for kings and for all that are in authority; that we may lead a quiet and

peaceable life in all godliness and honesty. [3] For this is good and acceptable in the sight of God our Saviour; [4] who will have all men to be saved and to come unto the knowledge of the truth.

We don't need to be fearful or worry, simply pray. For those who defy God, however, there is now a strong work of chastisement coming. Obey the Lord and spend time with him in honour and do what he says. The Lord's commands are not too hard. Bless the readers, by which I mean you, if you have read this. Bless all those who love our Lord Jesus Christ in sincerity. Amen.

NUCLEAR EXPLOSIONS, TWO DREAMS

First Dream

During the first weeks after receiving what we call 'the baptism of the Holy Spirit', I had a very profound dream. I was standing in a suburb somewhere near Perth City, and suddenly, there was an explosion and a great mushroom cloud above what I estimated was near Joondalup. I and others stood in awe and wonder, and my thoughts were to head south quickly to avoid the fallout. In a moment, another explosion went up south of us – this time, I'm thinking, near Fremantle. Before I had any more time to think, people all around me were melting away. In the split second before they had left, their faces were of incredulity of why those with me and I hadn't melted with them.

In the morning, a quote entered my mind that I could not remember ever reading: 'A thousand shall fall by your side and ten thousand by your right hand; but it shall not come nigh thee.' It was verse 8 of Psalms 91. I had not been reading the Bible for years, but as I had been touched by God, I had started again. It was so uplifting and encouraging to me as I had been very anxious in my teenage years as this was the mid-eighties. Since that time, God has delivered me out of many dangerous situations, including a serious car crash, falls from buildings, and other dangers I put myself in when I was young and foolish. He has never left me alone!

Second Dream

Approximately four years after the first dream, I had another nuclear explosion dream. I was standing in the front room of our little flat as it was in real life. I had recently been married, with our first child. I stood near one of the windows, which looked out over the hills. On a small table, a chronograph watch began to sound its alarm. The watch was a present for my eighteenth birthday, which, in real life, I had lost, but here it was, and instead of a normal LED crystal readout, it was gold. There, on the screen, was the symbol of a bomb coming down the screen, much like the early game watches people had in the eighties. It beeped as the bomb reached the bottom of the screen, and it portrayed an explosion at the bottom. It puzzled me as I never knew the watch could do this. Less than a moment passed when suddenly, the building shook, and a thunderous sound was everywhere. I looked out the window, and a massive mushroom cloud was high above us. There was also a crack of thunder and a brilliant flash like lightning. My mind went to the first dream, where it had a happy conclusion. This dream was oh so real, and it challenged me to consider how much I trusted God.

The next day, I shared the dream with my wife. There was no internet then. By coincidence, she had been reading an eyewitness account from a journalist who had been watching an atomic test. She said that my account was identical to that of the journalist's in terms of the attributes of the explosion. I do not say that this will definitely happen; however, there is a great possibility while mankind is so ready to unleash destruction on one another. I share that with you simply because it was shown to me, and it is a sobering reminder that we should all be aware of our responsibility to do our fair share of intercession, praying for both the lost and our leaders that we can live a peaceful and blessed life where all are safe and nurtured.

There is more to come. I cannot overstate the need of every person who can grasp the urgency of this time to ask God's forgiveness and pray for our nation and all the nations. There are more messages to come as I know God will say and do much in the near future.

Impossible?

Can an earthquake pursue a man? It will seek out the wicked.

Here are some scriptures from the Christian Bible for consideration:

[17] For God sent not his Son into the world to condemn the world but that the world through him might be saved. (John 3:17, KJV)

[9] The Lord is not slack concerning his promise as some men count slackness; but is longsuffering to us-ward, not willing that any should perish but that all should come to repentance. (2 Peter 3:9, KJV)

[8]having promise of the life that now is and of that which is to come. (1 Timothy 4:8 KJV)

[15] And the Lord God of their fathers sent to them by his messengers, rising up betimes and sending; because he had compassion on his people and on his dwelling place. [16] But they mocked the messengers of God and despised his words and misused his prophets until the wrath of the Lord arose against his people till there was no remedy. (2 Chronicles 36:15–16, KJV)

If you are reading this or if you can relay this message to any one of your family and acquaintances in trouble, know that God reigns supreme and that nothing can separate you from the love of God — no prison, no torture, no debt, no person of extreme abuse, nothing

[38] For I am persuaded, that neither death, nor life, nor angels, nor principalities, nor powers, nor things present, nor things to come, [39] Nor height, nor depth, nor any other creature, shall be able to separate us from the love of God, which is in Christ Jesus our Lord. Romans 8:38-39 KJV

Humble yourself; forgive your enemies. God has you on his radar, and his love is immeasurable, his mercy unending. Do not fear death. God will walk you through all the way whether you live long or short do not fear.

Read Psalm 23. I hope you don't need that advice, but truly, many are suffering from terror of one sort or another. Call to God. Never stop praying and returning to him. Even a thick concrete cell block cannot keep God out.

[7] And behold, the angel of the Lord came upon him and a light shined in the prison: and he smote Peter on the side and raised him up, saying, 'Arise . . . quickly.' And his chains fell off from his hands. [8] And the angel said unto him, 'Gird thyself and bind on thy sandals.' And so he did. And he saith unto him, 'Cast thy garment about thee and follow me.' [9] And he went out and followed him; and wist not that it was true which was done by the angel; but thought he saw a vision. [10] When they were past the first and the second ward, they came unto the iron gate that leadeth unto the city; which opened to them of his own accord: and they went out and passed on through one street; and forthwith, the angel departed from him. [11] And when Peter was come to himself, he said, 'Now I know of a surety that the Lord hath sent his angel and hath delivered me out of the hand of Herod and from all the expectation of the people of the Jews.' (Acts 12:7–11, KJV)

WHAT DOES JESUS LOOK LIKE?

It is common knowledge that Jesus was born as a Jew therefore he has that ancestry and look. There is a remarkable young woman who does the most phenomenal paintings. Her portrait of what she was inspired to paint as the image of Jesus is what I believe I saw in my dream. There was Jesus, far above the earth, surrounded by multitudes of people, modern-day people in ordinary clothes. There was Jesus in the middle of them all, leading the dancing. It was modern and joyful. If you can imagine this multitude covering the stratosphere like an immense dome over this part of the earth. All of these people for miles and miles were dancing in perfect congruity though miles apart but moving as one. The music was 'heavenly'. There is no sorrow in heaven, and therefore, the power of heaven is in enjoying our God in praise and worship that satisfies the most emaciated soul and lifts them, you, to a height that can only be described as divine and glorious. The hard part is living on earth after experiencing such delight, but that glory is always with us, and one can 'feel' it by living simply and spending time alone and in the quiet regularly. Early morning is a good time, four or five o'clock. This song is new every day, every minute, and is the place one can always find God's living water for their daily needs.

'Many have hoped for a turn around in the fortune and righteousness in the government and wellbeing of the USA. Those who know how to pray must do so unceasingly as this election will determine the future of not only the USA but many other nations.

Let God be the Lord of USA, in Jesus name. It is not about one man but about a nation choosing between good and evil, life and death. So choose life!

Get on you knees and pray for your nation and we will pray also.'

SIGNING OFF

For legal and intellectual property reasons, I will give no names or references. However, there is a book written by a Chinese man whose name rhymes with 'gun'. The title has to do with 'human paradise' (work that conundrum out – not hard). In that account is a modern-day story so similar to that of Peter. If you read further on in the Book of Acts, you will be delighted and encouraged. Miracles are just above your head. In these coming days, you will need them. The way of the Lord, at times, is hard, as stated at the beginning of this book, not because of God but because of those who hate him. Love everyone, including your enemies. When you are afraid and don't know what to do, pray. Ask Almighty God for His direction and protection but don't give in to hate and fear or greed. Pause to lift up your hands daily. Do look up, there is a Saviour above!

God bless you. Godspeed. The best is yet to come.

9 781669 888123